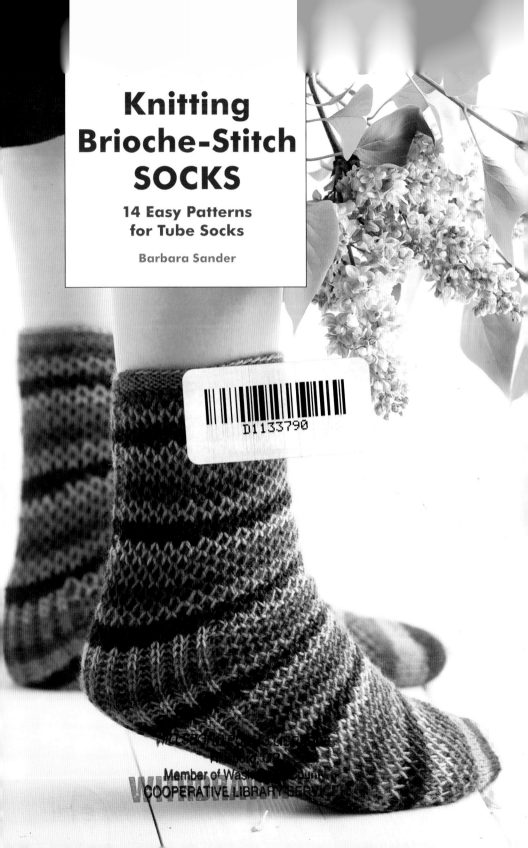

Knitting
Brioche-Stitch
SOCKS

14 Easy Patterns
for Tube Socks

Barbara Sander

Knitting Brioche-Stitch Socks:
14 Easy Patterns for Tube Socks
© 2011 by Barbara Sander

& C O M P A N Y

Martingale & Company®
19021 120th Ave. NE, Suite 102
Bothell, WA 98011 USA
www.martingale-pub.com

Martingale & Company Mission Statement

Dedicated to providing
quality products and service
to inspire creativity.

Credits

President & CEO ❖ Tom Wierzbicki
Editor in Chief ❖ Mary V. Green
Managing Editor ❖ Karen Costello Soltys
Design Director ❖ Stan Green
Technical Editor ❖ Ursula Reikes
Copy Editor ❖ Marcy Heffernan
Production Manager ❖ Regina Girard
Cover & Text Designer ❖ Stan Green
Photography ❖ frechverlag GmbH, 70499 Stuttgart;
           Lichpunkt, Michael Ruder,
           Stuttgart

The original German edition was published
as *Die Patentsocke*.

Copyright © 2010 frechverlag GmbH,
Stuttgart, Germany (www.frech.de)

This edition is published by arrangement with
Claudia Boehme Rights & Literary Agency,
Hannover, Germany (www.agency-boehme.com).

Acknowledgments

We thank Coats for their
support in this book
(www.coatsandclark.com).

Printed in China
16 15 14 13 12 11   8 7 6 5 4 3 2 1

**Library of Congress Cataloging-
in-Publication Data is available
upon request.**

ISBN: 978-1-60468-084-3
4870 5197 ⁶⁄₁₂

Contents

Introduction

Nothing keeps feet wonderfully warm like hand-knit socks. Once you've worn handmade socks, you'll never want to wear store-bought socks again, especially in winter.

Complicated techniques for knitting heels have discouraged many knitters from trying to make socks. That's over now, because this revolutionary sock design has no heel! The stretchy knitting technique used adapts perfectly to the shape of the foot, and it even lets the socks grow with children.

Knit in brioche stitch, these socks can be made in a very simple manner, but the design can easily be made more sophisticated by working two-color brioche stitch, combining brioche with other pattern stitches like garter or stockinette stitch, and by working with stripes. Using the size charts given on page 46, you can make any pattern in any size.

Let yourself be carried away by the diversity of patterns in the brave new world of socks!

Basic Instructions

The tube socks in this book are knit in the round in several variations of brioche stitch, which is very elastic. Because it's looser than stockinette stitch, and the knit fabric is quite stretchy, fewer stitches are cast on than with conventional socks.

Socks for All Sizes

All of the socks in this book can be knit in any size. See the charts on page 46 to choose the size you want to make and determine the correct number of stitches to cast on for that size.

For socks that are made entirely in brioche stitch, you only need to change the number of stitches to cast on and the total number of rounds to work for the desired length. For socks that have a different pattern on the instep with the sole worked in brioche stitch, cast on the number of stitches shown in the chart and work to the desired leg length. Then work the number of rounds specified in the chart for the instep and sole.

Yarn

To achieve the best results, use the yarn specified in each pattern. If this yarn isn't available to you, choose yarn that works up to the same gauge, preferably sock yarn, to guarantee the finished sock will be the right size and have the same wear properties as the sample shown. If you're making a sock larger than specified in the pattern, you may need to purchase additional yarn.

Working with Center-Pull Balls

Knitting is much easier when you knit with the tail of yarn pulled from the center of the skein. The yarn pulls easily from the center of the skein without tangling.

Starting Both Socks in the Same Place in the Colorway

Many specialty sock yarns have repeating color patterns or stripe sequences. When you join a new ball of yarn, make sure that the pattern is not interrupted and that you join the new ball of yarn at the correct place in the color sequence. This may mean unwinding a ball until you find the color repeat you need, and then winding a new ball from there.

Knitting Needles

Many different types of knitting needles are available today. There are needles made of metal, plastic, bamboo, and other special materials, such as rosewood. Try different types of needles to determine which material you prefer to work with, and be aware that needles of the same material but from different manufacturers may vary in quality. Choose the material that works with the yarn. Bamboo is very grabby, while plastic and rosewood are a little more slippery, and metal is very slippery.

Casting On

The long-tail cast on is used for the socks in this book.

1. To create a loop for the first stitch, hold the needle in your right hand and drape the long tail of yarn over the top of the needles so the tail is away from you (in the back) and the working yarn attached to the ball is near you (in the front). Cross the strands underneath the needles. Place the working yarn around your left index finger and the yarn tail around your left thumb. Grasp the strands in your palm.

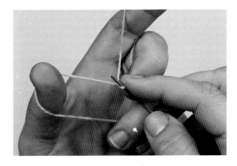

2. Pull the needle down a bit, until the two parts of the thumb yarn cross, and insert the needle from below into the thumb loop.

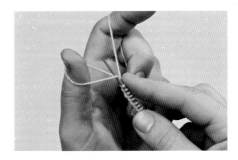

3. Draw the working yarn through the loop.

4. Pull your thumb out of the loop. You now have a new stitch on the needle. Reposition your thumb under the tail and your index finger under the working yarn, and tug gently to tighten the new stitch on the needle. Repeat the process until you have cast on the desired number of stitches.

Casting On over Two Needles
For brioche-stitch socks, it's particularly important to cast on very loosely. To achieve a nice, relaxed tension, work the cast on over two needles held together. Carefully pull the extra needle out before knitting the first round.

Basic Brioche Stitch in the Round

Individual patterns indicate whether to work over an even number or odd number of stitches.

Round 1
1. Knit one stitch.

2. Work a yarn over and slip a stitch at the same time: Bring the yarn to the front between the needles; then insert the right needle into the next stitch from right to left, as if to purl.

3. Slip the stitch purlwise onto the right needle; then bring the working yarn over the top of the needle to the back again. (The yarn over will lie across the slipped stitch.)

Repeat steps 1–3 around. This round is worked only once as a setup round.

Round 2

1. Work a yarn over and slip a stitch at the same time: Bring the yarn to the front between the needles; then insert the right needle into the next stitch from right to left, as if to purl.

Arranging Stitches on Double-Pointed Needles

For added clarity in the instructions, the needles are numbered starting with the working yarn at the beginning of the round, as shown below.

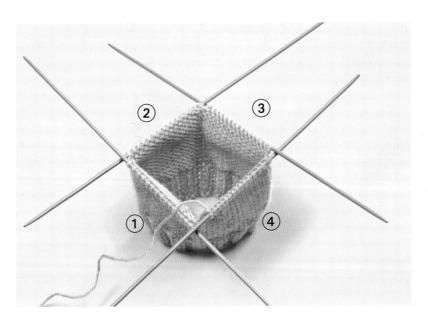

2. Slip the stitch purlwise onto the right needle; then bring the working yarn over the top of the needle to the back again. (The yarn over will lie across the slipped stitch.)

Round 3

1. Knit the next yarn over and stitch together.

3. Bring the yarn to the front between the needles and purl the next yarn over and the stitch together. You have one new yarn over/slip stitch pair and one new purl stitch on the right needle.

2. Work a yarn over and slip a stitch at the same time: Bring the yarn to the front between the needles; then insert the right needle into the next stitch from right to left, as if to purl.

Repeat steps 1–3 around.

3. Slip the stitch purlwise onto the right needle; then bring the working yarn over the top of the needle to the back again. (The yarn over will lie across the slipped stitch.)

Repeat steps 1–3 around.

Repeat rounds 2 and 3 for the basic brioche-stitch pattern. Every yarn over/slip stitch pair counts as one stitch. Every two rounds of brioche stitch counts as one round of knitting.

Gauge

Everyone knits at their own gauge—some rather loosely, others tightly. To avoid ending up with a sock that is too small or too big, you definitely must knit a gauge swatch.

Each pattern gives the number of stitches and rows in 4". So knit a rectangle that is at least 4½" for your swatch. When you measure your swatch, if you counted more stitches than required in 4", your knitting is too tight. Try again with larger needles. If you have fewer stitches than required, your gauge was too loose. Try again with smaller needles.

All of the brioche stitches in the socks are worked in the round. To knit gauge swatches, however, work the following stitch patterns back and forth.

Basic Brioche Stitch
Worked Back and Forth
Worked over an odd number of stitches

Row 1 (WS): K1 (selvage), *K1, (sl1 pw wyif, YO); rep from * to last 2 sts: K1, K1 (selvage).

Row 2: K1 (selvage), *(sl1 pw wyif, YO), knit the next YO and st tog; rep from * to last 2 sts, knit next YO and st tog, K1 (selvage).

Row 3: K1 (selvage), *knit the next YO and st tog, (sl1 pw wyif, YO); rep from * to last 2 sts, (sl1 pw wyif, YO), K1 (selvage).

Repeat rows 2 and 3 for pattern.

Half Brioche Stitch
Worked Back and Forth
Worked over an odd number of stitches

Row 1 (RS): K1 (selvage), *K1, (sl1 pw wyif, YO); rep from * to last 2 sts, K1, K1 (selvage).

Row 2: K1 (selvage), *P1, purl the next YO and st tog; rep from * to last 2 sts, P1, K1 (selvage).

Repeat rows 1 and 2 for pattern.

Decreases

The following decreases are used in this book.

Knit Two Together (K2tog)
With the working yarn held in back, insert the needle from left to right through *two loops* on the left needle

at once, and work them together as a regular knit stitch. You have decreased one stitch.

Knitting two stitches together to decrease one stitch

Purl Two Together (P2tog)

With the working yarn held in front, insert the needle from right to left through *two loops* on the left needle at once, and work them together as a regular purl stitch. You have decreased one stitch.

Purling two stitches together to decrease one stitch

Star Toe Shaping

To shape the toes if you're working in a size other than as specified in each pattern, first work 5 to 10 rounds of stockinette stitch with no shaping. For this star-shaped toe, you need an even number of stitches on each needle. After each decrease round, work the same number of rounds without shaping as the decrease round had stitches between decreases.

For example: If you have 48 stitches for the toe, arrange the stitches so you have 12 on each needle. Then work as follows:

Dec rnd 1: (K4, K2tog) around— 40 sts.

Knit 4 rnds.

Dec rnd 2: (K3, K2tog) around— 32 sts.

Knit 3 rnds.

Dec rnd 3: (K2, K2tog) around— 24 sts.

Knit 2 rnds.

Continue in this manner until only eight stitches remain, two on each needle. Break the yarn and use a tapestry needle to thread the tail through the last eight stitches. See photo on facing page.

The star decreasing method creates a rounded toe, as opposed to sock toes where decreases are worked only along the sides to create a more pointed sock toe.

Blocking Socks

Steam or wet your finished socks and put them onto a sock blocking form. Make sure you choose a sock blocking form in the appropriate size and let the socks dry completely before removing them, so they maintain the heel shaping. Sock blocking forms are available in various sizes from yarn shops and online knitting sites.

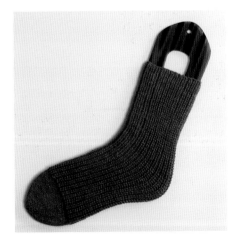

A sock blocking form helps create a nice smooth finished sock.

Basic Brioche-Stitch Socks

Size: Instructions are given for Women's Large/Men's Medium. These socks can be made in any size (see sizing chart on page 46).

Materials

2 balls of Regia 4-ply (75% wool, 25% nylon; 50 g; 229 yds) in color 1991 Light Gray Heather

Set of 5 size 2 US (2.75 mm) double-pointed needles

Gauge

24 sts and 60 rows = 4" over brioche st on size 2 needles

Pattern Stitches

Basic Brioche Stitch in the Round
Worked over an even number of sts

Rnd 1 (setup rnd): *K1, (sl1 pw wyif, YO); rep from * around.

Rnd 2: *(Sl1 pw wyif, YO), purl next YO and st tog; rep from * around.

Rnd 3: *Knit next YO and st tog, (sl1 pw wyif, YO); rep from * around.

Rep rnds 2 and 3 for patt.

Stockinette Stitch in the Round
Knit all rnds.

Leg/Foot

With 2 needles held tog, CO 48 sts loosely with even tension. Remove the 2nd needle. Divide sts evenly on 4 dpns and join to work in the rnd, being careful not to twist sts.

Rnd 1: (K1, P1) around.

Work in basic brioche st for 204 rnds.

Remember: 2 rnds of brioche equal 1 rnd of knitting, so count 102 sts in the column of knits. Or work rnds until desired length to toe.

Change to St st and work 8 rnds even.

Toe

Dec rnd 1: (K4, K2tog) around—40 sts.

Knit 4 rnds even.

Dec rnd 2: (K3, K2tog) around—32 sts.

Knit 3 rnds even.

Dec rnd 3: (K2, K2tog) around—24 sts.

Knit 2 rnds even.

Dec rnd 4: (K1, K2tog) around—16 sts.

Knit 1 rnd even.

Dec rnd 5: K2tog around—8 sts.

Break yarn and use a tapestry needle to thread tail through rem sts.

Weave in ends. Steam or wash socks, and then block on sock blocking forms until dry.

TOE-SHAPING TIP
Brioche-stitch socks can be worked with any type of toe shaping that you like!

Half Brioche-Stitch Socks

Size: Instructions are given for Women's Large/Men's Medium. These socks can be made in any size (see sizing chart on page 46).

Materials
2 balls of Regia 4-ply (75% wool, 25% nylon; 50 g; 229 yds) in color 2137 Jeans Heather

Set of 5 size 2 US (2.75 mm) double-pointed needles

Gauge
24 sts and 60 rows = 4" over brioche st on size 2 needles

Pattern Stitches

Half-Brioche Stitch in the Round
Worked over an even number of sts

Rnd 1: *K1, (sl1 pw wyif, YO); rep from * around.

Rnd 2: *K1, purl next YO and st tog; rep from * around.

Rep rnds 1 and 2 for patt.

Stockinette Stitch in the Round
Knit all rnds.

TRY A SELF-PATTERNING YARN
Using a self-patterning yarn can make even the simplest socks seem very sophisticated!

Leg/Foot
With 2 needles held tog, CO 48 sts loosely with even tension. Remove the 2nd needle. Divide sts evenly on 4 dpns and join to work in the rnd, being careful not to twist sts.

Rnd 1: (K1, P1) around.

Work in half-brioche st for 204 rnds. **Remember:** 2 rnds of brioche st equal 1 rnd of knitting, so count 102 sts in the column of knits. Or work rnds until desired length to toe.

Change to St st and work 8 rnds even.

Toe
Dec rnd 1: (K4, K2tog) around—40 sts.

Knit 4 rnds even.

Dec rnd 2: (K3, K2tog) around—32 sts.

Knit 3 rnds even.

Dec rnd 3: (K2, K2tog) around—24 sts.

Knit 2 rnds even.

Dec rnd 4: (K1, K2tog) around—16 sts.

Knit 1 rnd even.

Dec rnd 5: K2tog around—8 sts.

Break yarn and use a tapestry needle to thread tail through rem sts.

Weave in ends. Steam or wash socks, and then block on sock blocking forms until dry.

Interlocking Circles of Color

Skill level: Experienced ▰▰▰▰

Size: Instructions are given for Women's Medium/Men's Small. These socks can be made in any size (see sizing chart on page 46).

Materials

Regia 4-ply (75% wool, 25% nylon; 50 g; 229 yds)

A 1 ball in color 327 Pine Green

B 1 ball in color 2019 Lime

C 1 ball in color 2018 Ice Blue

D 1 ball in color 1988 Lavender

Set of 5 size 2 US (2.75 mm) double-pointed needles

Gauge

24 sts and 60 rows = 4" over 2-color brioche st on size 2 needles

Pattern Stitches

Two-Color Brioche Stitch in the Round
Worked over an even number of sts

Rnd 1 (setup rnd): With color 1, *K1, (sl1 pw wyif, YO); rep from * around.

Rnd 2: With color 2, *(sl1 pw wyif, YO), purl next YO and st tog; rep from * around.

Rnd 3: With color 1, *knit next YO and st tog, (sl1 pw wyif, YO); rep from * around.

Rep rnds 2 and 3 for patt.

Stockinette Stitch in the Round
Knit all rnds.

Stripe Pattern
Work 2-color brioche st in the rnd, changing stripes every 8 rnds as follows:

Stripe 1 (8 rnds): Work all rnds with B.

Stripe 2 (8 rnds): Work rnd 2 with B and rnd 3 with C.

Stripe 3 (8 rnds): Work all rnds with C.

Stripe 4 (8 rnds): Work rnd 2 with C and rnd 3 with D.

Stripe 5 (8 rnds): Work all rnds with D.

Stripe 6 (8 rnds): Work rnd 2 with D and rnd 3 with A.

Stripe 7 (8 rnds): Work all rnds with A.

Stripe 8 (8 rnds): Work rnd 2 with A and rnd 3 with B.

Rep stripes 1–8 (total 64 rnds) for patt.

Leg/Foot

With B and 2 needles held tog, CO 48 sts loosely with even tension. Remove the 2nd needle. Divide sts evenly on 4 dpns and join to work in the rnd, being careful not to twist sts.

Rnd 1: (K1, P1) around.

Work 2-color brioche st in stripe patt for 192 rnds (3 reps of stripe patt). **Remember:** 2 rnds of brioche st equal 1 rnd of knitting, so count 96 sts in the column of knits. Or work rnds until desired length to toe.

With A, change to St st and work 8 rnds even.

Toe

Dec rnd 1: (K4, K2tog) around—40 sts.

Knit 4 rnds even.

Dec rnd 2: (K3, K2tog) around—32 sts.

Knit 3 rnds even.

Dec rnd 3: (K2, K2tog) around—24 sts.

Knit 2 rnds even.

Dec rnd 4: (K1, K2tog) around—16 sts.

Knit 1 rnd even.

Dec rnd 5: K2tog around—8 sts.

Break yarn and use a tapestry needle to thread tail through rem sts.

Weave in ends. Steam or wash socks, and then block on sock blocking forms until dry.

TOE COLOR

If you make this sock in a different size, the sock may not be the correct length to end after the eighth stripe of the pattern before working the toe. Work the toe in whichever color you're using for your last stripe.

Modern Color Transitions

Skill level: Intermediate ◼◼◼▢

Size: Instructions are given for Women's Large/Men's Medium. These socks can be made in any size (see sizing chart on page 46).

Materials

A 1 ball of Regia 4-ply Color (75% wool, 25% polyamide; 50 g; 230 yds) in color 4536 Over Cassis

B 1 ball of Regia 4-ply (75% wool, 25% nylon; 50 g; 229 yds) in color 2020 Violet

C 1 ball of Regia Extra Twist Merino (75% superwash merino, 25% polyamide; 50 g; 231 yds) in color 9354 Violet

Set of 5 size 2 US (2.75 mm) double-pointed needles

Gauge

24 sts and 60 rows = 4" over brioche st on size 2 needles

CHANGING COLORS IN STRIPES

Yarn A is a self-striping yarn. The pattern looks more harmonious if you change the second yarn (B or C) at the same time that A starts a new color. This may mean that each stripe has a few less or a few more than 16 rounds.

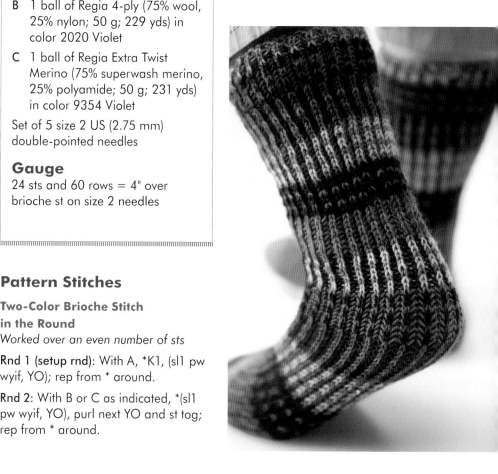

Pattern Stitches

Two-Color Brioche Stitch in the Round
Worked over an even number of sts

Rnd 1 (setup rnd): With A, *K1, (sl1 pw wyif, YO); rep from * around.

Rnd 2: With B or C as indicated, *(sl1 pw wyif, YO), purl next YO and st tog; rep from * around.

Rnd 3: With A, *knit next YO and st tog, (sl1 pw wyif, YO); rep from * around.

Rep rnds 2 and 3 for patt.

Stockinette Stitch in the Round
Knit all rnds.

Stripe Pattern
Work 2-color brioche st in the rnd, changing stripes every 16 rnds as follows:

Stripe 1 (16 rnds): Work rnd 2 in B and rnd 3 in A.

Stripe 2 (16 rnds): Work rnd 2 in C and rnd 3 in A.

Rep stripes 1 and 2 (a total of 32 rnds) for patt.

Leg/Foot
With A, beg with the desired portion of the colorway and 2 needles held tog, CO 48 sts loosely with even tension. Remove the 2nd needle. Divide sts evenly on 4 dpns and join to work in the rnd, being careful not to twist sts.

Rnd 1: (K1, P1) around.

Work 6 rnds in 2-color brioche st using A for all rnds; then work stripe patt for 208 rnds (6½ reps of stripe patt); for a total of 214 rnds. **Remember:** 2 rnds of brioche st equal 1 rnd of knitting, so count 107 sts in the column of knits. Or work rnds until desired length to toe.

With A, change to St st and work 4 rnds even.

Toe
Dec rnd 1: (K4, K2tog) around—40 sts. Knit 4 rnds even.

Dec rnd 2: (K3, K2tog) around—32 sts. Knit 3 rnds even.

Dec rnd 3: (K2, K2tog) around—24 sts. Knit 2 rnds even.

Dec rnd 4: (K1, K2tog) around—16 sts. Knit 1 rnd even.

Dec rnd 5: K2tog around—8 sts.

Break yarn and use a tapestry needle to thread tail through rem sts.

Weave in ends. Steam or wash socks, and then block on sock blocking forms until dry.

Sporty Jeans-Look Socks

SIZE CHANGES

To make this sock in a smaller size, work fewer than 20 rounds per stripe. For a larger size, work more than 20 rounds per stripe.

Skill level: Intermediate ◼◼◼▢

Size: Instructions are given for Women's Small. These socks can be made in any size (see sizing chart on page 46).

Materials
Regia 6-ply (75% wool, 25% nylon; 50 g; 137 yds per ball)

A 1 ball in color 2137 Jeans Heather

B 1 ball in color 1980 Gray Heather

Set of 5 size 4 US (3.5 mm) double-pointed needles

Gauge
18 sts and 54 rows = 4" over brioche st on size 4 needles

Pattern Stitches

Two-Color Brioche Stitch in the Round
Worked over an even number of sts

Rnd 1 (setup rnd): With color 1, *K1, (sl1 pw wyif, YO); rep from * around.

Rnd 2: With color 2, *(sl1 pw wyif, YO), purl next YO and st tog; rep from * around.

Rnd 3: With color 1, *knit next YO and st tog, (sl1 pw wyif, YO); rep from * around.

Rep rnds 2 and 3 for patt.

Stockinette Stitch in the Round
Knit all rnds.

Stripe Pattern
Work 2-color brioche st in the rnd, changing colors every 20 rnds as follows:

Stripe 1 (20 rnds): Work rnd 2 with A and rnd 3 with B.

Stripe 2 (20 rnds): Work rnd 2 with B and rnd 3 with A.

Rep stripes 1 and 2 (total 40 rnds) for patt.

Leg/Foot
With A and 2 needles held tog, CO 36 sts loosely with even tension. Remove the 2nd needle. Divide sts evenly on 4 dpns and join to work in the rnd, being careful not to twist sts.

Rnd 1: (K1, P1) around.

Work in 2-color brioche st in stripe patt for 180 rnds (4½ reps of stripe patt).

Remember: 2 rnds of brioche st equal 1 rnd of knitting, so count 90 sts in the column of knits. Or work rnds until desired length to toe.

With A, change to St st and work 6 rnds even.

Toe
Setup rnd: (K2tog, K7) around—32 sts.

Dec rnd 1: (K2, K2tog) around—24 sts. Knit 2 rnds even.

Dec rnd 2: (K1, K2tog) around—16 sts. Knit 1 rnd even.

Dec rnd 3: K2tog around—8 sts.

Break yarn and use a tapestry needle to thread tail through rem sts.

Weave in ends. Steam or wash socks, and then block on sock blocking forms until dry.

Cuddly Socks for Relaxing Moments

Skill level: Easy ◧ ■ ☐ ▷

Size: Instructions are given for Women's Medium/Men's Small. These socks can be made in any size (see sizing chart on page 46).

Materials

Regia Kids (40% wool, 60% nylon; 50 g; 137 yds)

A 3 balls in color 7853 Violet Kids

B 1 ball in color 7753 Susi Kids Color

Set of 5 size 3 US (3.25 mm) double-pointed needles

Gauge

18 sts and 46 rows = 4" over brioche st on size 3 needles

Pattern Stitches

Basic Brioche Stitch in the Round
Worked over an even number of sts

Rnd 1 (setup rnd): *K1, (sl1 pw wyif, YO); rep from * around.

Rnd 2: *(Sl1 pw wyif, YO), purl next YO and st tog; rep from * around.

Rnd 3: *Knit next YO and st tog, (sl1 pw wyif, YO); rep from * around.

Rep rnds 2 and 3 for patt.

Garter Stitch in the Round
Rnd 1: Knit.

Rnd 2: Purl.

Rep rnds 1 and 2 for patt.

Stripe Pattern
Stripe 1 (6 rnds): Work in B.

Stripe 2 (6 rnds): Work in A.

Leg/Foot

With A and 2 needles held tog, CO 40 sts loosely with even tension. Remove the 2nd needle. Divide sts evenly on 4 dpns and join to work in the rnd, being careful not to twist sts.

Rnd 1: Knit.

With A, work 30 rnds in garter st.

Change to basic brioche st and work 5 stripes (B, A, B, A, B), then cont working in brioche st with A for 122 rnds; a total of 152 rnds. **Remember:** 2 rnds of brioche st equal 1 rnd of knitting, so count 76 sts in the column of knits. Or work rnds until desired length to toe.

Change to garter st and work 8 rnds even.

Toe

Dec rnd 1: (K3, K2tog) around—32 sts.

Next 3 rnds: Purl, knit, purl.

Dec rnd 2: (K2, K2tog) around—24 sts.

Next 2 rnds: Purl, knit.

Dec rnd 3: (P1, P2tog) around—16 sts.

Next rnd: Knit.

Dec rnd 4: P2tog around—8 sts.

Break yarn and use a tapestry needle to thread tail through rem sts.

Weave in ends. Steam or wash socks, and then block on sock blocking forms until dry.

OTHER SIZES

When making this sock in a smaller size, work the stripe pattern with fewer rounds per color so the stripes are not too bold. For larger sizes, repeat the stripe pattern a few more times.

GIFTS FROM THE HEART
Hand-knit socks are a favorite gift. Tube socks made in stretchy brioche stitch are ideal, especially when you don't know the shoe size of the recipient.

Striking Two-Tone Ribs

Pattern Stitches

Two-Color Brioche Stitch in the Round
Worked over an even number of sts

Rnd 1 (setup rnd): With B, *K1, (sl1 pw wyif, YO); rep from * around.

Rnd 2: With A, *(sl1 pw wyif, YO), purl next YO and st tog; rep from * around.

Rnd 3: With B, *knit next YO and st tog, (sl1 pw wyif, YO); rep from * around.

Rep rnds 2 and 3 for patt.

Stockinette Stitch in the Round
Knit all rnds.

Leg/Foot

With B and 2 needles held tog, CO 48 sts loosely with even tension. Remove the 2nd needle. Divide sts evenly on 4 dpns and join to work in the rnd, being careful not to twist sts.

Rnd 1: (K1, P1) around.

Work in 2-color brioche st for 180 rnds. **Remember:** 2 rnds of brioche st equal 1 rnd of knitting, so count 90 sts in the column of knits. Or work rnds until desired length to toe.

With B, change to St st and work 8 rnds even.

Toe

Dec rnd 1: (K4, K2tog) around—40 sts.

Knit 4 rnds even.

Dec rnd 2: (K3, K2tog) around—32 sts.

Knit 3 rnds even.

Dec rnd 3: (K2, K2tog) around—24 sts.

Knit 2 rnds even.

Dec rnd 4: (K1, K2tog) around—16 sts.

Knit 1 rnd even.

Dec rnd 5: K2tog around—8 sts.

Break yarn and use a tapestry needle to thread tail through rem sts.

Weave in ends. Steam or wash socks, and then block on sock blocking forms until dry.

Skill level: Intermediate ■■■□

Size: Instructions are given for Women's Medium/Men's Small. These socks can be made in any size (see sizing chart on page 46).

Materials

2 balls of Regia 4-ply (75% wool, 25% nylon; 50 g; 229 yds) in color 33 Flannel Heather

Set of 5 size 2 US (2.75 mm) double-pointed needles

Gauge

24 sts and 60 rows = 4" over brioche st on size 2 needles

Pattern Stitches

Basic Brioche Stitch in the Round
Worked over an even number of sts

Rnd 1 (setup rnd): *K1, (sl1 pw wyif, YO); rep from * around.

Rnd 2: *(Sl1 pw wyif, YO), purl next YO and st tog; rep from * around.

Rnd 3: *Knit next YO and st tog, (sl1 pw wyif, YO); rep from * around.

Rep rnds 2 and 3 for patt.

Reverse Stockinette Stitch in the Round
Purl all rnds.

Leg/Foot

With 2 needles held tog, CO 52 sts loosely with even tension. Remove the 2nd needle. Divide sts evenly on 4 dpns and join to work in the rnd, being careful not to twist sts.

Rnd 1: (K1, P1) around.

Work in basic brioche st for 18 rnds (9 sts in the column of knits).

Rev St st Bands

Inc rnd: *K2, make 1; rep from * around—78 sts.

Work 11 rnds even in rev St st.

Dec rnd: *(Sl1 pw wyif, YO), purl next YO and st tog; rep from * around—52 sts.

Work 18 rnds in basic brioche st (9 sts in the column of knits).

Work 2 more rev St st bands separated by 18 rnds of brioche st (9 sts in the column of knits), then cont working on 52 sts in brioche st until you have 100 rnds (50 sts in the column of knits) after last rev St st band. Or work rnds until desired length to toe.

Change to rev St st and work 5 rnds even.

Toe

Setup rnd: (P2tog, P11) around—48 sts.

Purl 5 rnds even.

Dec rnd 1: (P4, P2tog) around—40 sts.

Purl 4 rnds even.

Dec rnd 2: (P3, P2tog) around—32 sts.

Purl 3 rnds even.

Dec rnd 3: (P2, P2tog) around—24 sts.

Purl 2 rnds even.

Dec rnd 4: (P1, P2tog) around—16 sts.

Purl 1 rnd even.

Dec rnd 5: P2tog around—8 sts.

Break yarn and use a tapestry needle to thread tail through rem sts.

Weave in ends. Steam or wash socks, and then block on sock blocking forms until dry.

Comfy Socks with Cuffs

Skill level: Experienced ● ■ ■ ▶

Size: Instructions are given for Women's Medium/Men's Small. These socks can be made in any size (see sizing chart on page 46).

Materials

2 balls of Regia 4-ply (75% wool, 25% nylon; 50 g; 229 yds) in color 2143 Linen Heather

Size 2 US (2.75 mm) straight needles

Set of 5 size 2 US (2.75 mm) double-pointed needles

Gauge

24 sts and 60 rows = 4" over brioche st on size 2 needles

Pattern Stitches

Basic Brioche Stitch in the Round
Worked over an even number of sts

Rnd 1 (setup rnd): *K1, (sl1 pw wyif, YO); rep from * around.

Rnd 2: *(Sl1 pw wyif, YO), purl next YO and st tog; rep from * around.

Rnd 3: *Knit next YO and st tog, (sl1 pw wyif, YO); rep from * around.

Rep rnds 2 and 3 for patt.

Tunisian Brioche Stitch
Worked back and forth over an odd number of sts

Row 1 (RS): K1 (selvage), *K1, (sl1 pw wyif, YO); rep from * to last 2 sts, K1, K1 (selvage).

Row 2 (WS): K1 (selvage), *K1, knit next YO and st tog; rep from * to last 2 sts, K1, K1 (selvage).

Rep rows 1 and 2 for patt.

Stockinette Stitch in the Round
Knit all rnds.

Cuff
Cuff is worked flat and sewn into a tube.

With straight needles, CO 55 sts and work in Tunisian brioche st for 8½" or desired cuff diameter.

BO all sts.

Shape cuff into a tube and sew center-back seam.

Leg/Foot
Sock sts are picked up around bottom edge of cuff.

With WS facing and dpns, PU 52 sts along bottom edge of cuff. Divide sts evenly on 4 dpns.

Work in basic brioche st for 140 rnds.

Remember: 2 rnds of brioche st equal 1 rnd of knitting, so count 70 sts in the column of knits. Or work rnds until desired length to toe.

Change to St st and work 5 rnds even.

Toe
Setup rnd: (K2tog, K11) around—48 sts.

Knit 5 rnds even.

Dec rnd 1: (K4, K2tog) around—40 sts.

Knit 4 rnds even.

Dec rnd 2: (K3, K2tog) around—32 sts.

Knit 3 rnds even.

Dec rnd 3: (K2, K2tog) around—24 sts.

Knit 2 rnds even.

Dec rnd 4: (K1, K2tog) around—16 sts.

Knit 1 rnd even.

Dec rnd 5: K2tog around—8 sts.

Break yarn and use a tapestry needle to thread tail through rem sts.

Weave in ends. Steam or wash socks, and then block on sock blocking forms until dry. Fold down cuff.

Netted Brioche-Stitch Socks

Skill level: Experienced ⬤ ■ ■ ◗

Size: Instructions are given for Women's Small. These socks can be made in any size (see sizing chart on page 46).

Materials

2 balls of Regia 4-ply (75% wool, 25% nylon; 50 g; 229 yds) in color 1841 Monte Carlo Big Stripes

Set of 5 size 2 US (2.75 mm) double-pointed needles

Gauge

24 sts and 60 rows = 4" over brioche st on size 2 needles

Pattern Stitches

Basic Brioche Stitch in the Round
Worked over an odd number of sts

Rnd 1 (setup rnd): *K1, (sl1 pw wyif, YO); rep from * to last st, K1.

Rnd 2: *(Sl1 pw wyif, YO), purl next YO and st tog; rep from * to last st, sl1 pw wyif, YO.

Rnd 3: *Knit next YO and st tog, (sl1 pw wyif, YO); rep from * to last st, knit next YO and st tog.

Rep rnds 2 and 3 for patt.

Garter Stitch in the Round
Rnd 1: Knit.

Rnd 2: Purl.

Rep rnds 1 and 2 for patt.

Stockinette Stitch in the Round
Knit all rnds.

Netted (or Honeycomb) Brioche Stitch in the Round
Worked over an even number of sts

Rnd 1 (setup rnd): *K1, (sl1 pw wyif, YO); rep from * around.

Rnd 2: *K2, wyib sl the next YO pw; rep from * around.

Rnd 3: *(Sl1 pw wyif, YO), purl next YO and st tog; rep from * around.

Rnd 4: *K1, wyib slip next YO pw, K1; rep from * around.

Rnd 5: *Purl next YO and st tog, (sl1 pw wyif, YO); rep from * around.

Rep rnds 2–5 for patt.

Leg/Foot

With 2 needles held tog, CO 48 sts loosely with even tension. Remove the 2nd needle. Divide sts evenly on 4 dpns and join to work in the rnd, being careful not to twist sts.

Rnd 1: Knit.

Work 5 rnds of garter st, then work in netted brioche st for 74 rnds.

On next rnd, set up patts for instep and sole as follows: Sl the first st from needle 2 onto needle 1. Beg working basic brioche st over the 23 sts on needles 1 and 4, and cont working netted brioche st as established over the sts on needles 2 and 3.

Cont in patts as established until you have worked a total of 180 rnds or until desired length to toe.

Rearrange sts so they are divided evenly on 4 dpns.

Change to St st and work 8 rnds even.

Toe

Dec rnd 1: (K4, K2tog) around—40 sts.

Knit 4 rnds even.

Dec rnd 2: (K3, K2tog) around—32 sts.

Knit 3 rnds even.

Dec rnd 3: (K2, K2tog) around—24 sts.

Knit 2 rnds even.

Dec rnd 4: (K1, K2tog) around—16 sts.

Knit 1 rnd even.

Dec rnd 5: K2tog around—8 sts.

Break yarn and use a tapestry needle to thread tail through rem sts.

Weave in ends. Steam or wash socks, and then block on sock blocking forms until dry.

Elegant Ombré Socks

Skill level: Intermediate ■■■□

Size: Instructions are given for Women's Medium/Men's Small. These socks can be made in any size (see sizing chart on page 46).

Materials

2 balls of Regia Hand-dye Effect (70% superwash wool, 25% nylon, 5% acrylic; 100 g; 462 yds) in color 6555 Agate

Set of 5 size 2 US (2.75 mm) double-pointed needles

Gauge

24 sts and 60 rows = 4" over brioche st on size 2 needles

Pattern Stitches

Basic Brioche Stitch in the Round
Worked over an odd number of sts

Rnd 1 (setup rnd): *K1, (sl1 pw wyif, YO); rep from * to last st, K1.

Rnd 2: *(Sl1 pw wyif, YO), purl next YO and st tog; rep from * to last st, sl1 pw wyif, YO.

Rnd 3: *Knit next YO and st tog, (sl1 pw wyif, YO); rep from * to last st, knit next YO and st tog.

Rep rnds 2 and 3 for patt.

Stockinette-Brioche Stitch in the Round
Worked over an even number of sts

Note that st patt varies from basic brioche st in that you knit next YO and st tog in rnd 2 rather than purl next YO and st tog.

Rnd 1 (setup rnd): *K1, (sl1 pw wyif, YO); rep from * around.

Rnd 2: *(Sl1 pw wyif, YO), knit next YO and st tog; rep from * around.

Rnd 3: *Knit next YO and st tog, (sl1 pw wyif, YO); rep from * around.

Rep rnds 2 and 3 for patt.

Garter Stitch in the Round
Rnd 1: Knit.

Rnd 2: Purl.

Rep rnds 1 and 2 for patt.

Stockinette Stitch in the Round
Knit all rnds.

Leg/Foot

With 2 needles held tog, CO 48 sts loosely with even tension. Remove 2nd needle. Divide sts evenly on 4 dpns and join to work in the rnd, being careful not to twist sts.

Work 4 rnds in garter st, then work in stockinette-brioche st for 74 rnds.

On the next rnd, set up patts for instep and sole as follows: Sl first st from needle 2 onto needle 1. Beg working basic brioche st over the 23 sts on needles 1 and 4, and cont working in stockinette-brioche st as established over sts on needles 2 and 3.

Cont in patt as established until you have worked a total of 192 rnds or until desired length to toe.

Rearrange sts so they are divided evenly on 4 dpns.

Change to St st and work 8 rnds even.

Toe

Dec rnd 1: (K4, K2tog) around—40 sts.

Knit 4 rnds even.

Dec rnd 2: (K3, K2tog) around—32 sts.

Knit 3 rnds even.

Dec rnd 3: (K2, K2tog) around—24 sts.

Knit 2 rnds even.

Dec rnd 4: (K1, K2tog) around—16 sts.

Knit 1 rnd even.

Dec rnd 5: K2tog around—8 sts.

Break yarn and use a tapestry needle to thread tail through rem sts.

Weave in ends. Steam or wash socks, and then block on sock blocking forms until dry.

MATCHING SOCKS

With self-striping and patterned yarns, the socks will be especially beautiful if you start the second sock in the same place in the colorway so both socks match.

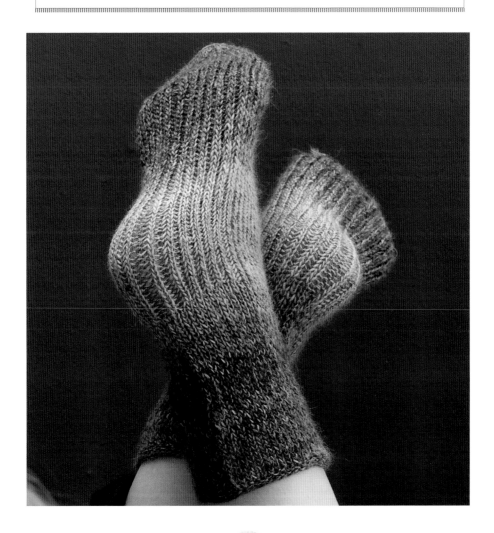

Color Play with Two-Tone Ribs

Size: Instructions are given for Women's X-Large/Men's Large. These socks can be made in any size (see sizing chart on page 46).

Materials

A   1 ball of Regia 4-ply (75% wool, 25% nylon; 50 g; 229 yds per ball) in color 1078 Cardinal

B   1 ball of Regia 4-ply Design Line (75% wool, 25% nylon; 50 g; 231 yds per ball) in color 4355 Landscape Celebration

Set of 5 size 2 US (2.75 mm) double-pointed needles

Gauge

24 sts and 60 rows = 4" over brioche st on size 2 needles

Pattern Stitches

Two-Color Basic Brioche Stitch in the Round
Worked over an odd number of sts

Rnd 1 (setup rnd): With A, *K1, (sl1 pw wyif, YO); rep from * to last st, K1.

Rnd 2: With B, *(sl1 pw wyif, YO), purl next YO and st tog; rep from * to last st, (sl1 pw wyif, YO).

Rnd 3: With A, *knit next YO and st tog, (sl1 pw wyif, YO); rep from * to last st, knit next YO and st tog.

Rep rnds 2 and 3 for patt.

Two-Color Stockinette-Brioche Stitch in the Round
Worked over an even number of sts

Rnd 1 (setup rnd): With B, *K1, (sl1 pw wyif, YO); rep from * around.

Rnd 2: With A, *(sl1 pw wyif, YO), knit next YO and st tog; rep from * around.

Rnd 3: With B, *knit next YO and st tog, (sl1 pw wyif, YO); rep from * around.

Rep rnds 2 and 3 for patt.

Garter Stitch in the Round
Rnd 1: Knit.

Rnd 2: Purl.

Rep rnds 1 and 2 for patt.

Leg/Foot

With B and 2 needles held tog, CO 52 sts loosely with even tension. Remove 2nd needle. Divide sts evenly on 4 dpns and join to work in the rnd, being careful not to twist sts.

Work 4 rnds in garter st, then work in 2-color stockinette-brioche st for 74 rnds.

On next rnd, set up patterns for instep and sole as follows: Sl first st from needle 2 onto needle 1. Beg working 2-color basic brioche st over 23 sts on needles 1 and 4, and cont working 2-color stockinette-brioche st as established over sts on needles 2 and 3.

Cont in patts as established until you have worked a total of 216 rnds or until desired length to toe.

Rearrange sts so they are divided evenly on 4 dpns.

With A, change to garter st and work 8 rnds even.

Toe

Setup rnd: (K2tog, K11) around—48 sts.

Next 5 rnds: Purl, knit, purl, knit, purl.

Dec rnd 1: (K4, K2tog) around—40 sts.

Next 4 rnds: Purl, knit, purl, knit.

Dec rnd 2: (P3, P2tog) around—32 sts.

Next 3 rnds: Knit, purl, knit.

Dec rnd 3: (P2, P2tog) around—24 sts.

Next 2 rnds: Knit, purl.

Dec rnd 4: (K1, K2tog) around—16 sts.

Next rnd: Purl.

Dec rnd 5: K2tog around—8 sts.

Break yarn and use a tapestry needle to thread tail through rem sts.

Weave in ends. Steam or wash socks, and then block on sock blocking forms until dry.

Tone-on-Tone with Texture

Skill level: Easy ◖■□▷

Size: Instructions are given for Women's Medium/Men's Small. These socks can be made in any size (see sizing chart on page 46).

Materials

Regia 4-ply (75% wool, 25% nylon; 50 g; 229 yds per ball)

A   2 balls in color 44 Medium Gray Heather

B   1 ball in color 2066 Black

Set of 5 size 2 US (2.75 mm) double-pointed needles

Gauge

24 sts and 60 rows = 4" over brioche st on size 2 needles

Pattern Stitches

Two-Color Brioche Stitch in the Round
Worked over an odd number of sts

Rnd 1 (setup rnd): With A, *K1, (sl1 pw wyif, YO); rep from * to last st, K1.

Rnds 2 and 4: With A, *(sl1 pw wyif, YO), purl next YO and st tog; rep from * to last st, (sl1 pw wyif, YO).

Rnd 3: With B, *knit next YO and st tog, (sl1 pw wyif, YO); rep from * to last st, knit next YO and st tog.

Rnd 5: With A, work as rnd 3.

Rep rnds 2–5 for patt.

Two-Color Garter Stitch in the Round
Rnds 1 and 2: With A, purl.

Rnd 3: With B, knit.

Rnd 4: With A, knit.

Rep rnds 1–4 for patt.

**Reverse Stockinette Stitch
in the Round**
Purl all rnds.

Leg/Foot

With A and 2 needles held tog, CO 48
sts loosely with even tension. Remove
2nd needle. Divide sts evenly on 4
dpns and join to work in the rnd, being
careful not to twist sts.

Work in 2-color garter st for 69 rnds.

On next rnd, set up patt for instep and
sole as follows: Sl first st from needle
2 onto needle 1. Beg working 2-color
brioche st over 23 sts on needles 1 and
4, and cont working 2-color garter st
as established over sts on needles 2
and 3.

Cont in patt as established until you
have worked a total of 192 rnds or until
desired length to toe.

Rearrange sts so they are divided
evenly on 4 dpns.

With A, change to rev St st and work 8
rnds even.

Toe

Dec rnd 1: (P4, P2tog) around—40 sts.

Purl 4 rnds even.

Dec rnd 2: (P3, P2tog) around—32 sts.

Purl 3 rnds even.

Dec rnd 3: (P2, P2tog) around—24 sts.

Purl 2 rnds even.

Dec rnd 4: (P1, P2tog) around—16 sts.

Purl 1 rnd even.

Dec rnd 5: P2tog around—8 sts.

Break yarn and use a tapestry needle
to thread tail through rem sts.

Weave in ends. Steam or wash socks,
and then block on sock blocking forms
until dry.

Subtle Two-Tone Combination

Skill level: Easy ◖■□▷

Size: Instructions are given for Women's Medium/Men's Small. These socks can be made in any size (see sizing chart on page 46).

Materials

Regia 4-ply (75% wool, 25% nylon; 50 g; 229 yds per ball);
A 1 ball in color 2000 Royal Blue
B 1 ball in color 2004 Dove Gray
Set of 5 size 2 US (2.75 mm) double-pointed needles

Gauge

24 sts and 60 rows = 4" over brioche st on size 2 needles

Pattern Stitches

Two-Color Brioche Stitch in the Round
Worked over an odd number of sts

Rnd 1 (setup rnd): With A, *K1, (sl1 pw wyif, YO); rep from * to last st, K1.

Rnd 2: With B, *(sl1 pw wyif, YO), purl next YO and st tog; rep from * to last st, (sl1 pw wyif, YO).

Rnd 3: With A, *knit next YO and st tog, (sl1 pw wyif, YO); rep from * to last st, knit next YO and st tog.

Rep rnds 2 and 3 for patt.

One-Color Garter Stitch in the Round
Rnd 1: Knit.

Rnd 2: Purl.

Rep rnds 1 and 2 for patt.

Two-Color Garter Stitch in the Round
Rnd 1: With B, knit.

Rnd 2: With A, purl.

Rep rnds 1 and 2 for patt.

Stockinette Stitch in the Round
Knit all rnds.

Leg/Foot

With A and 2 needles held tog, CO 48 sts loosely with even tension. Remove 2nd needle. Divide sts evenly on 4 dpns and join to work in the rnd, being careful not to twist sts.

Work 6 rnds in 1-color garter st, then work in 2-color garter st for 74 rnds.

On next rnd, set up patts for instep and sole as follows: Sl first st from needle 2 onto needle 1. Beg working 2-color brioche st over the 23 sts on needles 1 and 4, and cont working 2-color garter st as established over the sts on needles 2 and 3.

Cont in patts as established until you have worked a total of 192 rnds or until desired length to toe.

Rearrange sts so they are divided evenly on 4 dpns.

With A, change to St st and work 8 rnds even.

Toe

Dec rnd 1: (K4, K2tog) around—40 sts.
Knit 4 rnds even.

Dec rnd 2: (K3, K2tog) around—32 sts.
Knit 3 rnds even.

Dec rnd 3: (K2, K2tog) around—24 sts.
Knit 2 rnds even.

Dec rnd 4: (K1, K2tog) around—16 sts.
Knit 1 rnd even.

Dec rnd 5: K2tog around—8 sts.

Break yarn and use a tapestry needle
to thread tail through rem sts.

Weave in ends. Steam or wash socks,
and then block on sock blocking forms
until dry.

Sock Sizing Charts

Socks with Regia 4-Ply

US Sizing	Child's Small	Child's Medium	Child's Large	Child's X-Large	Women's X-Small	
Cast on	40	40	40	44	44	
Stitches per needle	10	10	10	11	11	
Leg length	1¾"	2½"	2½"	3"	3"	
Sole and instep rounds	96	104	110	116	122	
Total rounds to toe	128	144	152	168	176	

Socks with Regia 6-Ply

US Sizing	Child's Small	Child's Medium	Child's Large	Child's X-Large	Women's X-Small	
Cast on	28	32	32	36	36	
Stitches per needle	7	8	8	9	9	
Leg length	1¾"	2½"	2½"	3"	3"	
Sole and instep rounds	86	92	98	104	110	
Total rounds to toe	116	130	136	152	158	

Socks with Regia Kids

US Sizing	Child's Small	Child's Medium	Child's Large	Child's X-Large	Women's X-Small	
Cast on	28	32	32	36	36	
Stitches per needle	7	8	8	9	9	
Leg length	1¾"	2½"	2½"	3"	3"	
Sole and instep rounds	76	82	88	92	96	
Total rounds to toe	102	114	122	134	140	

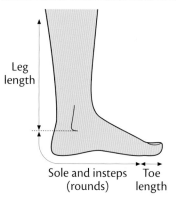

Leg length

Sole and insteps (rounds)   Toe length

1️⃣ Sock, Fingering, Baby

3️⃣ DK, Light Worsted

Women's Small	Women's Medium/ Men's Small	Women's Large/Men's Medium	Women's X-Large/ Men's Large	Men's X-Large	Men's 2X
48	48	48	52	52	56
12	12	12	13	13	14
3¾"	3¾"	3¾"	4¼"	4¼"	4¼"
128	134	140	144	150	158
188	200	212	224	230	238

Women's Small	Women's Medium/ Men's Small	Women's Large/Men's Medium	Women's X-Large/ Men's Large	Men's X-Large	Men's 2X
36	40	40	40	44	44
9	10	10	10	11	11
3¾"	3¾"	3¾"	4¼"	4¼"	4¼"
114	120	126	130	134	140
170	180	190	200	204	212

Women's Small	Women's Medium/ Men's Small	Women's Large/Men's Medium	Women's X-Large/ Men's Large	Men's X-Large	Men's 2X
36	40	40	40	44	44
9	10	10	10	11	11
3¾"	3¾"	3¾"	4¼"	4¼"	4¼"
102	108	112	114	120	126
150	160	170	180	184	190

Useful Information

Abbreviations

beg	begin(ning)
BO	bind off
cont	continue(ing)(s)
CO	cast on
dec	decrease(ing)(s)
dpn(s)	double-pointed needle(s)
g	gram(s)
inc	increase(ing)(s)
K	knit
K2tog	knit 2 stitches together—1 stitch decreased
mm	millimeter(s)
P	purl
P2tog	purl 2 stitches together—1 stitch decreased
patt	pattern(s)
PU	pick up and knit
pw	purlwise
rem	remain(ing)
rep(s)	repeat(s)
rev St st(s)	reverse stockinette stitch(es)
rnd(s)	round(s)
sl	slip
sl1	slip 1 stitch
St st(s)	stockinette stitch(es)
st(s)	stitch(es)
tog	together
WS	wrong side
wyib	with yarn in back
wyif	with yarn in front
yd(s)	yard(s)
YO(s)	yarn over(s)

Skill Levels

Each project in this book has been assigned a skill level. Those skill levels indicate the type of knitting you'll encounter in that project

◄■□□ **Easy:** Projects using basic repetitive stitch patterns.

◄■■□ **Intermediate:** Projects using more than one stitch pattern with some color changes.

◄■■► **Experienced:** Projects using more than one stitch pattern, and two-color stitch patterns.

Metric Conversions

Yards x .91 = meters

Meters x 1.09 = yards

Grams x .035 = ounces

Ounces x 28.35 = grams